WESTMINSTER SCHOOLS

SMYTHE GAMBRELL
LIBRARY

PRESENTED BY

Laura Smith   1988

T.T.

YOUR EYES

Joan Iveson-Iveson

Illustrated by Bill Donohoe

The Bookwright Press
New York · 1985

All About You

Your Eyes
Your Teeth

Acknowledgments

Sally and Richard Greenhill 6, 7, 11; Preben Kristensen 5, 17; Wayland Picture Library 12, 15; J. Merrett 20, 22

First published in the United States in 1985 by
The Bookwright Press
387 Park Avenue South
New York, NY 10016

Second impression 1987

First published in 1985 by Wayland (Publishers) Limited
61 Western Road, Hove
East Sussex BN3 1JD, England
© 1985 Wayland (Publishers) Limited

ISBN 0–531–18014–X
Library of Congress Catalog Card Number: 84–73572

Printed by G. Canale & C.S.p.A., Turin, Italy

Contents

What are eyes for?

All the time you are awake you are using your eyes. They are very special and seeing is perhaps your most important sense. You have four other senses: hearing, taste, touch and smell. There are many things you couldn't do if you couldn't see. Can you think of some?

Everyone's eyes work in the same way, like
very fast cameras, but they all look a little
different. Some people have big, round eyes,
others have small, slanting eyes. You can see
the difference between the girls' eyes in the
pictures. Eyes are different colors too. Some
people have to wear glasses or **contact lenses**
to help them to see better.

Good protection

When you look in the mirror you can only see the very small front part of your eyes. The rest is hidden inside your bony skull, fitting into two holes called **eye sockets**. Because your eyes are so precious they need great care. The hard skull protects the parts inside your head. The boy in the picture has a black eye, but it is only the part around his eye that is bruised.

Your eyebrows keep rainwater or sweat from running into your eyes, and your eyelashes trap bits of dust. If something gets into your eye, your eyelids blink very fast to push it out again. In the top of your eye sockets are **tear glands** that make salty, clean **tears** which you blink across your eyes all the time to keep them clean, wet and protected from germs. In the corners of your eyes your **tear ducts** drain away the tears into your nose. That is why your nose runs when you cry.

The different parts

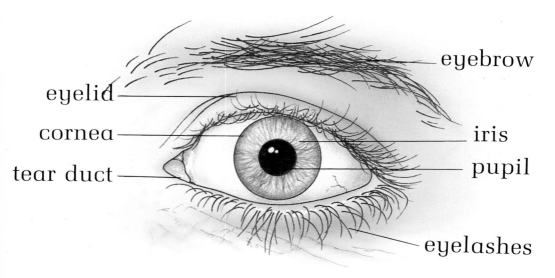

eyebrow

eyelid

cornea

iris

tear duct

pupil

eyelashes

The white part of the eye that you see is a tough cover that protects your round eyeball. Part of it stretches over the middle of your eye, where it bulges out. This bit is called the **cornea** and it is clear, to let light through. The colored ring it covers is called the **iris**, and the black hole in the middle of the iris is the **pupil**. Light gets inside your eye through this black hole.

8

This drawing shows you the insides of your eyes. Behind each pupil is a **lens,** which is clear so that light can get through. Special muscles squeeze the rubbery lens to make it fatter, or pull it to make it thinner. This is called **focusing**, and helps you see something clearly. Behind the lens is a space filled with clear jelly that keeps the eyeball round. At the back of the eye there is a thin lining called the **retina**. The retina is joined to the big **optic nerve** that carries the picture you see to your brain.

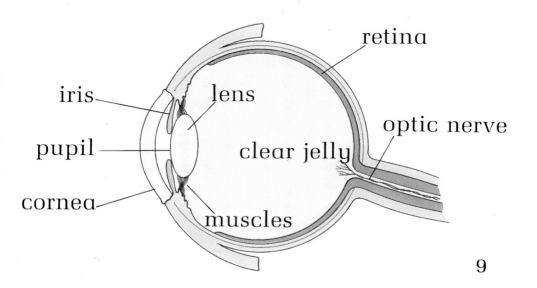

iris

lens

retina

pupil

clear jelly

optic nerve

cornea

muscles

How light gets in

Light gets into your eyes through the black holes called pupils. If you look in the mirror and almost close your eyes, your pupils will get bigger. Quickly open your eyes wide and you will see your pupils getting smaller.

When it is dark your pupils get bigger to let in more light. When it is bright, they close up

to keep too much light from getting in, which would hurt your eyes.

If you look closely at your irises you will see tiny dark lines, or rays. These are muscles that pull the irises open, making the pupils bigger. Other muscles are in rings and they push the iris shut, making the pupils smaller.

Bright light can be uncomfortable. The boy in the picture is wearing a hat to shade his eyes from strong sunlight.

How you see

When you look at an object your eyes take in all its different colors and shapes. They do this by collecting the **light rays** coming from it. The drawing shows what happens inside your eye when you look at something. The light rays from the object travel through the clear cornea, through the pupil, then through the lens. The lens is squeezed, or flattened, by its muscles into the right shape to focus the

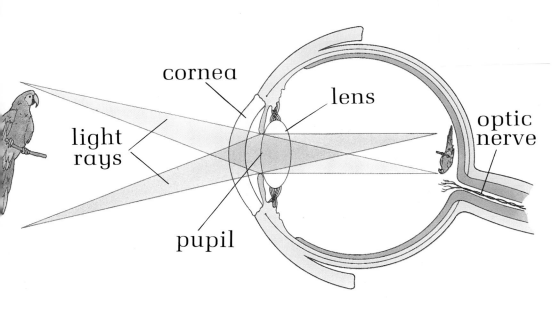

cornea

lens

optic
nerve

light
rays

pupil

light rays on the retina. The light rays cross over at the lens and make a tiny, upside-down picture on the retina.

The retina is made of cells called **rods**, which pick up black and white light, and **cones**, which pick up colors. The big optic nerve carries what the eye sees to the brain to be turned the right way up.

13

Seeing problems

If your eyeball is too long or too short, you will be either nearsighted or farsighted. Being nearsighted means that objects far away look blurred. The light rays coming from them meet in front of the retina instead of exactly on it. If you are farsighted, objects close-to look

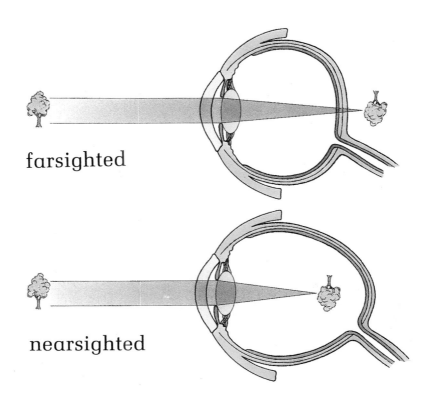

farsighted

nearsighted

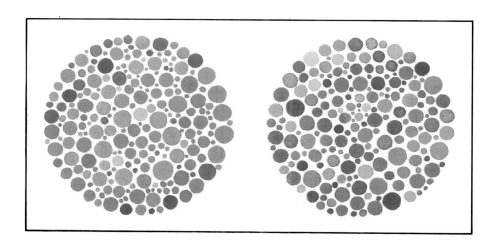

blurred, because the light rays meet behind the retina. To see clearly, you need glasses or contact lenses with specially shaped lenses. These bend the light rays so they land exactly on the retina.

Can you see the numbers in the circles? People who are **color-blind** cannot usually see red, green or blue. This is because they may not have enough cones.

In dim light only the rods work. So at night you only see in shades of black, white and gray.

The color of your eyes

Everyone's eyes are different colors. They can be blue, green, gray or violet, hazel, brown or almost black. The color is made of pigments, which everyone has in their bodies. The pigments mix together like paints to make a certain color.

The color of your eyes comes from your

parents. If they both have brown eyes you will probably have brown eyes. If they both have blue eyes you will probably have blue eyes. If one parent has brown eyes and one parent has blue eyes, their children will nearly always have brown eyes. Brown is the stronger color. Dark-skinned people usually have brown eyes, like the Indian boy in the picture. Some babies are born with blue eyes that slowly change color as they get older.

Blindness

Close your eyes and tie a dark scarf over them. Then sit still for a few minutes in black darkness, and you will know what it feels like to be blind. Blind people have to use their other senses of hearing, touch, taste and smell

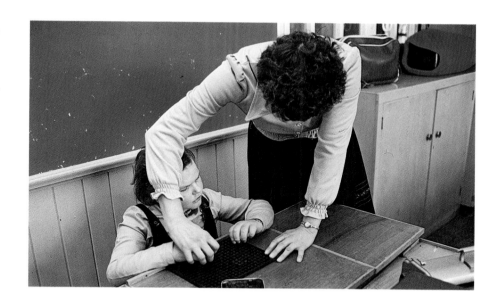

to help them.

Some people are born blind and have no idea of what the world around them looks like. Other people go blind when they are older and can remember what they are missing.

Blind people can read using touch. Books in a special language called **braille**, have raised dots in different patterns, instead of letters. The girl in the picture is being taught how to read braille.

Visiting the optometrist

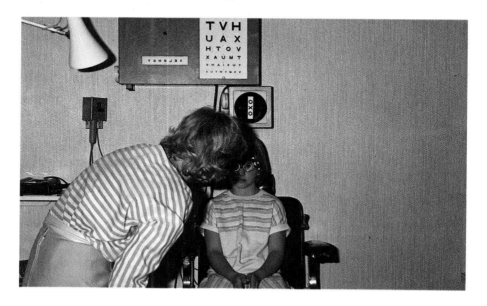

You have probably had your eyes tested at school. If you need glasses you must visit the **optometrist**, who is specially trained to test your eyes and fit you with glasses.

At the optometrist's you sit in a special chair in a dark room. Only the things you look at are lit up. First, the optometrist checks inside your eyes with a special instrument called an **ophthalmoscope**, which shines a light through your pupils. You can see it in the drawing. Then you must read different-sized letters on a chart. This tests how well you can see. The optometrist also tests you for other things like color blindness, and how far to either side you can see without moving your eyes.

Some people choose contact lenses instead of glasses. These are tiny, round, clear lenses that fit over the cornea.

Looking after your eyes

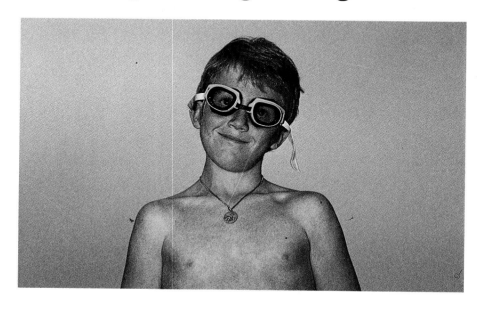

The chlorine in the water in swimming pools can sometimes make your eyes sore. The boy in the picture is wearing goggles to protect his eyes when he is swimming.

Your eyes are very precious and need to be looked after. The list on these pages will help you remember how best to take care of them.

Have your eyes checked regularly.
If you have glasses you should wear them,
and have them checked every six months.
Eat food like milk, cheese, liver, eggs, and
especially carrots, which have vitamin A in
them. This helps to keep your eyes healthy.
If you are doing woodwork, or anything where
bits of dust are flying around, wear a mask to
keep the dust from going into your eyes.
If you do get something in your eye, and
blinking doesn't get rid of it, ask an adult to
help.
Try not to rub your eyes with your fingers,
especially if they are itchy or sore. Use a clean
tissue instead. This keeps germs from getting
in your eyes.
If you get headaches or can't see some things
clearly, tell your parents or teacher. You
might need glasses.
Don't make your eyes tired. Always read in a
good light coming from behind you.

Word list

Braille Special printing for blind people.

Color-blind Not able to tell the difference between red and green.

Cones Color seeing cells.

Contact lenses Rounded, clear plastic lenses placed over the cornea to help you see better.

Cornea The clear outer layer of your eyeball.

Focusing The squeezing or flattening of the lens to get a clear picture of an object.

Iris The colored part of the eye.

Lens The clear, rounded part inside the eye which helps you see an object clearly.

Light rays Straight, narrow beams of light.

Pupil The black center of the eye.

Optometrist A person trained to test your eyes and fit you with glasses.

Optic nerve This carries messages from your eye to your brain.

Retina The layer of cells at the back of the eye.

Rods Cells that see black and white light.

Tears Clean, salty drops of liquid that protect your eyes.

Tear ducts Where the tears drain out of your eyes into the back of your nose.

Tear glands Where the tears are made.

Index